Praise for *In the La*

"Forché's stately stanzas—her writing is nev   :-porter, Gloria Emerson as filtered through the eyes of Elizabeth Bishop or Grace Paley. Free of jingoism but not of moral gravity, Forché's work questions—when it does question—how to be or to become a thinking, caring, communicating adult. Taken together, Forché's five books . . . are about action: memory as action, vision and writing as action. She asks us to consider the sometimes unrecognized, though always felt, ways in which power inserts itself into our lives and to think about how we can move forward with what we know. History—with its construction and its destruction—is at the heart of *In the Lateness of the World*. . . . In [it] one feels the poet cresting a wave—a new wave that will crash onto new lands and unexplored territories."

—Hilton Als, *The New Yorker*

"Auden once wrote that poetry makes nothing happen, but in Forché's work, her lifelong commitment to poetry and the poetic utterance, we see how poetry can transform. Both *What You Have Heard Is True* and *In the Lateness of the World* are essential reading not only for anyone interested in poetry, but in the world we live in."

—*Independent* (Ireland)

"*In the Lateness of the World* is a testament to the aftermath of human culture . . . Forché's belief that it is the poet's responsibility to speak truth from these wounded cities creates poems that are sometimes difficult to reckon with even as they soar in moments of unexpected beauty."   —*The New York Times Book Review*

"An undisputed literary event."   —Craig Morgan Teicher, NPR

"The title of Carolyn Forché's new collection seems prophetic. Seventeen years in the making, *In the Lateness of the World* is an act of witness, going repeatedly into the darkness of death and loss. . . . Forché's almost incantatory way with image produces a strange tone, spellbound but also emotionally charged, in which time and place shift and blur—because we're all implicated."   —*The Guardian* (London)

"Anyone familiar with Forché's work knows that her poetry of witness moves well beyond stunning imagery, having broad implications for the lives it hopes to remember and the readers it hopes to implore. . . . There is in these poems a sense of responsibility: to the fullness of lives unnecessarily unbound; to poetry and its insistence on meaning; to attention and action, no matter the cost." —*World Literature Today*

"Carolyn Forché's fourth poetry collection, *Blue Hour*, appeared in 2003, and her readers have longed for the next ever since. It's hard to imagine any poetry book worth a wait of seventeen years. Forché's new collection, *In the Lateness of the World*, is worth more." —*Sojourners*

"[A] genuinely moving consideration of 'ours and the souls of others, who glimmer beside us / for an instant . . . radiant with significance,' communicating an urgent and affecting vision." —*Publishers Weekly* (starred review)

"Carolyn Forché is a master poet, one whose work has always spoken to the ethical urgency of our day. This new book is filled with such poems. Open the book on the poem called 'Boatman,' for instance, and you will be under a spell. The piece is as fresh as morning news and as timeless as a parable. Yet, I feel there is also something new in this book, an even larger scope, a prophetic mode. . . . This long-awaited collection is not to be missed." —Ilya Kaminsky, author of *Deaf Republic*

"We are unfixed here to time or to place; we are nowhere, but we are in a meticulously particular nowhere. The rocks, pebbles, and stones are far from concepts, metaphors, or abstractions. The specificity almost takes on an animism, a beating element that Forché captures in a crescendoing, rhythmic drama, spiked with occasional shards of human agency." —John Washington, *The Nation*

"Throughout her career, Forché has forged poems of witness, and she does so here with beauty and lyricism." —*Library Journal*

"Someone who bears witness, who offers the possibility of this watershed moment, is not asking the listener for any favors. They are giving listeners an opportunity to no longer live in denial, in ignorance, or in indifference: to become someone who is truly present in the world and who stands by their perceptions and convictions, and to be truly oneself in the company of others. *Lateness*, thus, is no longer about looking at the world. Each poem is an invitation to be *in* the world and with the lives that we are in the process of destroying." —*The Massachusetts Review*

PENGUIN BOOKS

IN THE LATENESS
OF THE WORLD

Carolyn Forché is an American poet, translator, and memoirist. Her books of poetry are *Blue Hour*, *The Angel of History*, *The Country Between Us*, and *Gathering the Tribes*. Her memoir, *What You Have Heard Is True*, was published by Penguin Press in 2019. In 2013, Forché received the Academy of American Poets Fellowship given for distinguished poetic achievement. In 2017, she became one of the first two poets to receive the Windham-Campbell Prize. She is a University Professor at Georgetown University. She lives in Maryland with her husband, photographer Harry Mattison.

ALSO BY CAROLYN FORCHÉ

POETRY

Blue Hour
The Angel of History
The Country Between Us
Gathering the Tribes

PROSE

What You Have Heard Is True

EDITED BY CAROLYN FORCHÉ

Poetry of Witness: The Tradition in English 1500–2001
Against Forgetting: Twentieth-Century Poetry of Witness

IN THE LATENESS
OF THE WORLD

———

Carolyn Forché

PENGUIN BOOKS

PENGUIN BOOKS

An imprint of Penguin Random House LLC

penguinrandomhouse.com

First published in the United States of America by Penguin Press,
an imprint of Penguin Random House LLC, 2020
Published in Penguin Books 2021

ISBN 9780525560425 (paperback)

THE LIBRARY OF CONGRESS HAS CATALOGED THE HARDCOVER EDITION AS FOLLOWS:
Names: Forché, Carolyn, author.
Title: In the lateness of the world / Carolyn Forché.
Description: New York : Penguin Press, 2020.
Identifiers: LCCN 2019037457 (print) | LCCN 2019037458 (ebook) |
ISBN 9780525560401 (hardcover) | ISBN 9780525560418 (ebook)
Subjects: LCGFT: Poetry.
Classification: LCC PS3556.O68 I5 2020 (print) |
LCC PS3556.O68 (ebook) | DDC 811/.54—dc23
LC record available at https://lccn.loc.gov/2019037457
LC ebook record available at https://lccn.loc.gov/2019037458

Printed in the United States of America
1   3   5   7   9   10   8   6   4   2

Designed by Cassandra Garruzzo

for Harry and Sean

and in memory of the others

To those, finally, whose roads of ink and blood go through words and men.

And, most of all, to you. To us. To you.

EDMOND JABÈS

CONTENTS

IN THE LATENESS
OF THE WORLD

These are your stones, assembled in matchbox and tin,

collected from roadside, culvert, and viaduct,

battlefield, threshing floor, basilica, abattoir—

stones, loosened by tanks in the streets,

from a city whose earliest map was drawn in ink on linen,

schoolyard stones in the hand of a corpse,

pebble from Baudelaire's *oui*,

stone of the mind within us

carried from one silence to another,

stone of cromlech and cairn, schist and shale, hornblende,

agate, marble, millstones, ruins of choirs and shipyards,

chalk, marl, mudstone from temples and tombs,

stone from the silvery grass near the scaffold,

stone from the tunnel lined with bones,

lava of a city's entombment, stones

chipped from lighthouse, cell wall, scriptorium,

paving stones from the hands of those who rose against the army,

stones where the bells had fallen, where the bridges were blown,

those that had flown through windows, weighted petitions,

feldspar, rose quartz, blue schist, gneiss, and chert,

fragments of an abbey at dusk, sandstone toe

of a Buddha mortared at Bamian,

stone from the hill of three crosses and a crypt,

from a chimney where storks cried like human children,

stones newly fallen from stars, a stillness of stones, a heart, altar and boundary stone, marker and vessel, first cast, load and hail,

bridge stones and others to pave and shut up with,

stone apple, stone basil, beech, berry, stone brake,

concretion of the body, as blind as cold as deaf,

all earth a quarry, all life a labor, stone-faced, stone-drunk

with hope that this assemblage of rubble, taken together, would become

a shrine or holy place, an ossuary, immovable and sacred

like the stone that marked the path of the sun as it entered the human

dawn.

THE BOATMAN

We were thirty-one souls, he said, in the gray-sick of sea
in a cold rubber boat, rising and falling in our filth.
By morning this didn't matter, no land was in sight,
all were soaked to the bone, living and dead.
We could still float, we said, from war to war.
What lay behind us but ruins of stone piled on ruins of stone?
City called "mother of the poor" surrounded by fields
of cotton and millet, city of jewelers and cloak-makers,
with the oldest church in Christendom and the Sword of Allah.
If anyone remains there now, he assures, they would be utterly alone.
There is a hotel named for it in Rome two hundred meters
from the Piazza di Spagna, where you can have breakfast under
the portraits of film stars. There the staff cannot do enough for you.
But I am talking nonsense again, as I have since that night
we fetched a child, not ours, from the sea, drifting face-
down in a life vest, its eyes taken by fish or the birds above us.
After that, Aleppo went up in smoke, and Raqqa came under a rain
of leaflets warning everyone to go. Leave, yes, but go where?
We lived through the Americans and Russians, through Americans
again, many nights of death from the clouds, mornings surprised
to be waking from the sleep of death, still unburied and alive
with no safe place. Leave, yes, we'll obey the leaflets, but go where?
To the sea to be eaten, to the shores of Europe to be caged?
To *camp misery* and *camp remain here*. I ask you then, where?

You tell me you are a poet. If so, our destination is the same.

I find myself now the boatman, driving a taxi at the end of the world.

I will see that you arrive safely, my friend, I will get you there.

They have cut off the water in the sinking metropolis.
Do not wash clothes! Bathe only with small buckets!

Meanwhile, cisterns on the roofs of the rich send it
singing through the pipes of the better houses.

There is the sound of applause, it is the clap of wings
just before doves enter the darkness of the dovecote.

Then a quiet comes. The sirens die down. Security gates
slam shut. It is like night. We are waiting to breathe again.

The gamecocks are forced to fight with knives taped to their feet.
This is illegal. So is everything else and there is never enough.

The logs are fed little by little into the mouths of the clay ovens.
Many songbirds have been roasted by the heavens.

Motor scooters flock through the streets, a murmuration.
Crossing like starlings the skies. It is a matter of thirst.

They transport the cocks in baskets covered by plastic bags—
their entire lives tethered to the ground, trapped in wicker.

Until they are angry enough. Roof to roof in the conclaves,
cistern to cold cistern. They have seen to it.

The rich will have what they want. Is this a relief?
The last cloud is empty. The first death reason enough.

REPORT FROM AN ISLAND

Sea washes the sands in a frill of salt and a *yes* sound.
We lie beneath palms, under the star constellations

of the global south: a cross, a sword pointing upward.
Through frangipani trees, a light wind. Bats foraging.

Foreigners smoke the bats out by burning coconuts,
calling this *the bat problem*. Or they set out poisonous fruit.

The gecko hides under a banana leaf. So far nothing is said.
A gecko mistaken for a bird that sings in the night.

It is no bird. A healer blows smoke into the wound.
Sees through flesh to a bone once broken.

In the sea, they say, there is an island made of bottles and other trash.
Plastic bags become clouds and the air a place for opportunistic birds.

One and a half million plastic pounds make their way there every hour.
The pellets are eggs to the seabirds, and the bags, jellyfish to the turtle.

So it is with diapers, shampoo, razors and snack wrappers, soda rings
and six-pack holders. Even the sacks to carry it all home flow to the sea.

Wind has lofted the water into a distant city, according to news reports:
most of that city submerged now, with fish in the streets.

It is no bird. The man hasn't sold any of his carved dolphins.
Geckos don't sing. The vendor of sarongs hasn't sold a single one.

Prau, the boats are called throughout this archipelago.
Spider-looking. Soft-motored. Waiting at dawn.

Geckos can't blink, so they lick their own eyes to keep them wet. Their bite
is gentle, they eat mealworms and crickets. This is why no crickets sing.

No one talks about it, but people look to the sea
toward where the plane went down. There is time to imagine:

one hundred eighty-nine souls buckled to their seats on the seafloor,
the wind too much for the plane, the gecko now at the door.

After the earthquake, people moved into the family tombs.
Many graves now have light and running water.

Others live at the dumps in trash cities, where there is work sorting
plastic, metal, glass, tantalum from cell phones and precious earths.

This work is slow. A low hum of ordinary life drills into the mind
like the sound of insects devouring a roof. There is no hope for it.

There is only the sea and its *yes*, lights in the city of the dead,
and a plastic island that must from space appear to be a palace.

THE LAST PUPPET

Moonlight taps on the puppet maker's hut, the tip of a brush
touching hide, light falling into water from an egret's wings

like tears on glass. Stones dusted with ash. Taps as if someone were there,
attempting to wake us up. A bell ringing in a tomb of cloud.

This debris is the puppet maker's house, taken by a sudden wind.
A storm like the future, filled with pigs, trees, cars, and something

no one should wish to see. Fires on the seafloor. Burnt weather.
The once-soft air embalmed in salt. As if God said it.

They kill the snake, drain its blood into a glass of liquor
along with its still-beating heart. Not everyone does this.

You drink it, and later you chew and chew the strong muscle of snake.
In another place, the blood of fruit bats is given without the heart.

No one knows the difference this makes.

Souls have their own world. The corpse its bone cage.
Nothing but fire everywhere the fire finds air.

There are no hides left, this is the last puppet.
The puppet maker lifts it to the light and has it speak

a language it will never speak again, its shadow finding the shadow on the wall of no one else. Then he puts a last song in its mouth.

Souls have their own world. They are the descendants of clouds. Take this puppet to America. Hold it to the light.

THE LIGHTKEEPER

A night without ships. Foghorns calling into walled cloud, and you
still alive, drawn to the light as if it were a fire kept by monks,
darkness once crusted with stars, but now death-dark as you sail inward.
Through wild gorse and sea wrack, through heather and torn wool
you ran, pulling me by the hand, so I might see this for once in my life:
the spin and spin of light, the whirring of it, light in search of the lost,
there since the era of fire, era of candles and hollow wick lamps,
whale oil and solid wick, colza and lard, kerosene and carbide,
the signal fires lighted on this perilous coast in the Tower of Hook.
You say to me, Stay awake, be like the lens maker who died with his
lungs full of glass, be the yew in blossom when bees swarm, be
their amber cathedral and even the ghosts of Cistercians will be kind
        to you.
In a certain light as after rain, in pearled clouds or the water beyond,
seen or sensed water, sea or lake, you would stop still and gaze out
for a long time. Also, when fireflies opened and closed in the pines,
and a star appeared, our only heaven. You taught me to live like this.
That after death it would be as it was before we were born. Nothing
to be afraid. Nothing but happiness as unbearable as the dread
from which it comes. Go toward the light always, be without ships.

No matter how light it was or wet the fields, and whether or not the horses
from the stable down the road had broken their fence and were grazing

near our windows as horses in a dream, Anna would be gone, out
pounding the earth with her pronged hoe. She never woke me, although I
    slept

beside her, like sleeping near a hill wrapped in house-silk. Her teeth floated
in water on the nightstand where she kept her spectacles, this woman who

crossed, as a girl of my age, in the hold of a ship for weeks, lowering
her bucket of night soil by rope, then, from the sea-rinsed bucket, pouring

seawater over herself on the lower deck where bathing was permitted.
The salt stiffened her hair and burned her eyes, but she was clean.

It isn't what they tell you, pisklę—calling me the name of a little bird that
    sings
too much. If there were no cattle, horses, or sheep to be sold, they would
    take

people whose passage had been paid and whose forfeit put up. Our papers
were in order, and we had the passage and forfeit to board. They gave us

drinking water, but shut off all water at night. Two weeks of the rocking
boat and stink of buckets, all of us asleep on planks. Such rise and fall, such

pitch of the ship! But some nights on deck, holding the rails for all her life,
she said she ploughed the sea as she once had the fields, and into the
   furrows

of light went the seeds and the black-winged waters fell upon them.

The city of your childhood rises between steppe and sea, wheat and light,
white with the dust of cockleshells, stargazers, and bones of pipefish,
city of limestone soft enough to cut with a hatchet, where the sea
unfurls and acacias brought by Greeks on their ships
turn white in summer. So yes, you remember, this is the city you lost,
city of smugglers and violinists, chess players and monkeys,
an opera house, a madhouse, a ghost church with wind for its choir
where two things were esteemed: literature and ships, poetry and the sea.
If you return now, it will not be as a being visible to others, and when
you walk past, it will not be as if a man had passed, but rather as if
someone had remembered something long forgotten and wondered why.
If you return, your father will be alive to prepare for you
his mint-cucumber soup or give you the little sweet called *bird's milk*,
and after hours of looking with him for his sandals lost near the sea,
you visit again together the amusement park where
your ancestors are buried, and then go home to the apartment house
built by German prisoners of war, to whom your father gave bread,
which you remember surprised you. You take the tram to a stop
where it is no longer possible to get off, and he walks
with you until he vanishes, still holding in his own your invisible hand.

March. The Neva still white, crisp as communion, and as we walk
its bridges, steadying ourselves on the glaze, tubes of ice
slide from the gutter-spouts to the astonishment of dogs, some of whom
have not seen spring before, while others pretend not to remember,
and a woman bends over her late potatoes, sorting and piling, and you say
"in this house lived a friend of my father who was killed" and
"in that house lived another, and in this, a very bad poet no longer known."
We come to the synagogue and go in, as far back as a forgotten holiness,
where, we are told, you can whisper into the wall and be heard on the other
     side.
But the rabbi doesn't know you are deaf. We whisper into the wall to please
     him.
A sign in Cyrillic asks for donations, and in exchange we apparently buy
dozens of matzos wrapped in paper. *There are only a hundred*
of us left in the city. While we are here, a fisherman waits on the river,
seated with a bucket beside him, his line in the hole, but in the last hour
water has surrounded his slab of ice, so unbeknownst
he is floating downstream, having caught nothing, cold and delirious
with winter thoughts, as they all are and were, and as for rescue,
no one will come. It is spring. The Neva, white and crisp as communion.

We stand at the casement window of Pushkin's Lycée.

These are the desks where Pushkin wrote, his chalkboards, his astrolabe.

Snow falls from here into the past and vanishes on golden minarets.

Snow recedes from the birches. A lesson writes itself in winter chalk:

On the day Michelangelo died in Rome, Galileo was born in Pisa.

Isaac Newton was born the year Galileo died. When they searched for

the poet Kabir, they found nothing beneath his shroud but a sprig of
    jasmine.

Man is like the statue whispering about the marble chiseled from his
    mouth.

You are the guardian of this statue, standing in your silent world.

The year Isaac Newton died, there was a barn fire during a puppet show.

Kabir says all corpses go to the same place, and the world has fallen

in love with a dream. This life is not the same as your other life.

We are here now in one of the shrines of the silver poets.

You are one of the silver. The snow is a white peacock in a Russian poem.

THE LOST SUITCASE

So it was with the suitcase left in front
of the hotel—cinched, broken-locked,
papered with world ports, carrying what
mattered until then, when turning your back
to cup a match it was taken, and the thief,
expecting valuables, instead found books written
between wars, gold attic-light, mechanical birds singing,
and the chronicle of your country's final hours.
What, by means of notes, you hoped to become:
a noun on paper, paper *dark with nouns*:
swallows darting through a basilica, your hands up
in smoke, a cloud about to open over the city, pillows
breathing shallowly where you had lain, a ghost
in a hospital gown, and *here* your voice,
principled, tender, soughing through
a fence woven with pine boughs:
Writing is older than glass but younger
than music, older than clocks or porcelain but younger than rope.
Dear one, who even in speaking is silent,
for years I have searched, usually while asleep,
when I have found the suitcase open, collecting snow,
still holding your vade mecum of the infinite,
your dictionary of the no-longer-spoken,
a commonplace of wounds casually inflicted,
and the slender ledger of truly heroic acts.

Gone is your atlas of countries unmarked by war,

absent your manual for the preservation of hours.

The incunabulum is lost—both your earliest book

and a hatching place for your mechanical birds—

but the collection of aperçus having to do

with *light laying its eggs in your eyes* was found,

along with the prophecy that *all mass murders were early omens.*

In an antique bookshop, I found your catechism of atrophied faiths,

so I lay you to rest without your Psalter,

nor the monograph wherein you state your most

unequivocal and hard-won proposition:

that everything must happen but to whom doesn't matter.

Here are your books, as if they were burning.

Be near now, and wake to tell me who you were.

LAST BRIDGE

Andreanska, you were with him
in his final hours and I give you that,
speaking the language understood only
in the kitchen of childhood: for you,
a lamplit tongue spoken in tomato gardens
and prison camps by those sent away
and those who let them be sent, so many
words for *no one* and *nothing*,
until history came for them too
with its years of industry and waste,
a tram pulling black smoke behind itself.

These are the suitcases manufactured in
"communist times," from balsa and tin.
Here are the books, ink on vellum, sold
by hoodlums on the black market.
We must have crossed the bridge a dozen
times those nights, but—can you imagine?—
alone, with no one from whom to borrow a match.

There appeared a Russian deserter
"from Afghan war," who drew caricatures
for small change but never drew our likeness.
And some nights there was singing beneath
stone angels, but we were otherwise alone.

Svetko's memories were of the scent of garlic
fields beside the river, and of riding in the basket
of his father's bicycle along its banks. On the night
of the invasion there was a radio, and red-starred jeeps
that would become white-starred jeeps in the West.
Svetko, with his friends, turned the street signs
around, and by mistake the enemy marched into Austria.

So, it is over, you tell me. When he closed
his eyes, there were swans. You took his hand
on the last bridge and made him laugh.
You have my yes, Andreanska.

ELEGY FOR AN UNKNOWN POET

You who were apart, wanderer, stranger, who bent down in winter
for the lost glove of another, you are *ein Fremder* on earth
as if you had been written toward us. Listen: bells! You are sheltered
once again in the stillness of childhood, where the slow river remains,
rain singing from a gutter-spout, wet bottles, misted grillwork.

Apartness gathers the music of solitude as if it were a glass viola.
Bells ring that are and are not, and the soul is left wandering in the blue
    night.
You are the one watching, the one dreaming this, the homeless one left
    behind.
The soul has departed. Thinking, alone with your thoughts,
the poverty of waking life, here where it nears the eternal.

A man stood behind you holding a knife. You walked into the lake until
    only
your hat could be seen. The dead began *to wander quietly in the hall of stars.*
Your sister took her life. And then you couldn't bear the gaze of others.
What you could bear, and for long hours, were *the star-filled eyes of a toad.*
I am your translator. Pity me. It is impossible to slip *ein Fremder*
into the mouth of another.

Last summer I went with you to the crematorium.
We said poems and covered your body with gloves and roses.
I know that you are dead. Why do you ask and ask *what can be done?*

Black is the color of footsteps, frost, stillness, and tears.
It modifies branches and wings. Blue appears as cloud, flower, ice.
Deer stepping from the forest are also blue. A river is green,
but green as well are *flecks of decomposition*. Silver, the blossoming
poppies, a wind's voice, faces of the unborn.

The living, you say, appear unreal to you, as if they were on fire.
Yet the living gaze at the dead, imploring them to appear.
Why? you ask. The living are oblivious to what they are,
measuring time as the flickering of day and night.

Brown are the cesspools, rafters, and shadows; golden the day,
candles, and a tent of stars, ivory the hands and limbs of lovers,
purple a night wind, nostrils, and snails. A skiff is red, as are
wolf and wound. Yellow are the walls of summer.
Sleep is white, as is sickness, shirt, and revenant.

What is left us then but darkness? Oneself is always dark and near.

LETTER TO A CITY UNDER SIEGE

Turning the pages of the book you have lent me of your wounded city,
reading the braille on its walls, walking beneath ghost chestnuts
past fires that turn the bullet-shattered windows bronze,
flaring an instant without warming the fallen houses
where you sleep without water or light, a biscuit tin between you,
or later in the café ruins, you discuss all night the burnt literature
borrowed from a library where all books met with despair.
I wanted to give your notes back to you, to be
printed in another language, not yours or mine but a tongue
understood by children who make bulletproof vests out of cardboard.
We will then lie down in the cemetery where violets grew in your
   childhood
before snipers fired on the city using gravestones for cover.
Friend, absent one, I can tell you that your tunnel is still there,
mud-walled and hallowed of earth, dug for smuggling
oranges into the city—oranges!—bright as winter moons by the
   barrow-load.
So let's walk further up the street, to the hill where one is able to see
the city woven in fog, roofs filled with sky, uprooted bridges,
and a shop window where a shard of glass hangs over the spine of a book.
The library burns on page sixty, as it burns in all the newspapers of the world,
and the clopping of horses' hooves isn't the sound of clopping horses.
From here a dog finds his way through snow with a human bone.
And what else, what more? Even the clocks have run out of time.
But, my good friend, the tunnel! There is still a tunnel for oranges.

TRAVEL PAPERS

Au silence de celle qui laisse rêveur.
To the silence of the one who sets us dreaming.

RENÉ CHAR

1.

By boat we went to Seurasaari, where
the small fish were called *vendace.*
There a man blew a horn of birch wood
toward the nightless sea.

Still voice. Fire that is no fire.
Ahead years unknown to be lived—

2.

Bells from the tower in the all-at-once, then
one by one, hours. Outside
(so fleetingly) ourselves—

3.

In a still mirror, in a blue *within*
where this earthly journey dreaming
itself begins,

4.

thought into being from the hidden to the end of the visible.

5.

Mountains before and behind,
heather and lichen, yarrow, gorse,
then a sea village of chartreuse fronds.

Spent fuel, burnt
wind, mute swans.

6.

We drove the birch-lined
highway from Dresden
to Berlin behind armored
cars in late afternoon,
nineteenth of June, passing
the black cloud of a freight
truck from Budapest.

Through disappearing
villages, past horses grazing vanished fields.

7.

The year before you died, America
went to war again on the other
side of the world.

This is how the earth becomes,
you said, a *grotto of skeletons.*

8.
In the ruins of a station: a soaked
bed, broken chairs, a dead coal stove.

9.
White weather, chalk, and basalt,
puffins, fuchsia, and history shot
through with particles
of recognition: this one
wetted down with petrol then
set alight, that one taking
forty rounds, this other
found eleven years later in a bog.

10.
In the station house, imaginary
maps, smoke chased by wind, a registry
of arrivals, the logs of ghost
ships, and a few prison
diaries written on tissue paper.

11.
Do you remember the blue-leaved lilies?
The grotto, the hoarfrost, the frieze?

Through the casements of glass handblown
before the war, a birch tree lets snow drop
through its limbs onto other birches. Birch twigs
in wind through glass.

12.
Who were we then? Such
a laughter as morning peeled
its light from us!

13.
You said the cemeteries were full in a voice
like wind plaiting willows—fields in bloom
but silent without grasshoppers or bees.
What do you want then? You with your
neverness, your unknown, your
book of things, you
with once years ahead to be lived.

14.

Your father believes he took you
with him, that you are
in an urn beside your sleeping mother,
but I am still writing with your hand,
as you stand in your still-there of lighted words.

15.

Such is the piano's sadness and the rifle's moonlight.
Stairwells remember, as do doors, but windows do not—

do not, upon waking, gaze out a window
if you wish to remember your dream.

16.

An ache of hope that you will come back—
the cawing flock is not your coming.

17.

Did you float toward Salzburg? A wind
in the mustard fields?—or walk instead
beside me through the asylum in Kraków?
Hours after your death you seemed
everywhere at once like the swifts at twilight.

Now your moments are clouds
in a photograph of swifts.

18.
In the hour held
open between day and night under
the meteor showers of Perseid
we held each other for the last time.

Dead, you whispered *where is the road?*

There, through the last of the sentences, just there—
through the last of the sentences, the road—

THE REFUGE OF ART

*I am thinking of aurochs and angels, the secret of durable
pigments . . . the refuge of art.*

VLADIMIR NABOKOV

In an atelier once a shoe factory, an artist paints walls,
cromlechs, and cairns with pigmented stone-dust:
dolmens with markings from an unknown past,
horses chiseled in chalk on bluestone,
a huntsman's frieze in Paleolithic time.
Slate tiles light his vigil over stags in flight,
bison stampeding, wild aurochs with lyre-shaped
horns, horses galloping his walls, and upon them
serpents, spirals, lozenges, and stars.
In the dawn of humanity, children built passage tombs
for the dead: stone hives in earth for the hum of spirit.
At solstice still, the sun enters their chambers precisely
for seventeen minutes. Certain years also the moon.
Wintering swans fly over as the stars hiss out.
In hollow pits the dead repose, bones whitening
in utter dark, where not even bats sing, and until
seen from the air by pilots during the Great War,
the domes slept, round and risen in the fields.
They also saw their own jeweled cities, their chess villages,
quilts of crops, and snake of rivers, snow wounded
by wire not seen before, and after the war,
the pilots led engineers to the fields of the domes.

At first no one knew what they were. Nothing was known.
Not that the builders would have been children to them,
nor why they toiled their lives moving stones
for the sun to slip through at a winter dawn,
lighting the spirals, stars, and lozenges
that the artist now transcribes along with wild aurochs,
bison, and the ancient horse. It is not known why
he paints them, standing as he does in a slate blindness—
only that with time, he might decipher a message regarding
aurochs, bison and spirals, lozenges and stars.

A ROOM

There is, on the wall, a scroll of rice paper and silk,
where sixty years ago a monk, after grinding bamboo
ash and the glue of fish bones into a stick, rubbed
the stick into stone and water, brushing a moment
of light from mind to paper. The brush was the cloud
that rains water and ink and nothing it touches can be erased.
On the floor, there is a rug woven from memory
of wool shorn toward the end of spring after the animals
are washed in the river. Its red is from insects that lived
in the bark of oaks, its green the green of fungus
on mulberry trees, its language unknown:
crosses, arrows, the repetition of houses and shoes.
The table near the window was a girl's dowry chest,
with a wooden statue of Saint Dominic missing an arm,
and a Chinese couple in jade on pedestals of scholar-stone,
he stroking his long beard, hiding a sword behind his back,
she with an unopened lotus bloom over her shoulder,
two small Buddhas carried by hand from Hangzhou.
The blue crystal eggs were blown, then etched by a diamond cutter
who sold them in a city known for its nine-hundred-day siege.
A young man brought the coffee service from a souk:
six glass cups and a silver pot that chimes against a tray beside
books with the chapters *Sauntering*, *Reading*, *Fencing*,
and *Idea of Necessary Connexion*, warning us against
attributing to objects the internal sensations

they occasion, such as joy at finding the scroll after taking
shelter in a shop on an afternoon lit with fire pots, or relief
that the rug, soaked in the floodwaters that later destroyed
the house, was, in the end, saved by the snow it collected
on a winter night, its memory and the red
of its insects intact, along with, by coincidence, the dowry chest,
the saint, the Chinese couple, Buddhas, and blue eggs,
coffee service, and books chosen at random, as our moments are,
ours and the souls of others, who glimmer beside us
for an instant, here by chance and radiant with significance.

THE GHOST OF HEAVEN

1.

Sleep to sleep through thirty years of night,
a child herself with child,
for whom we searched

through here, or there, amidst
bones still sleeved and trousered,
a spine picked clean, a paint can,
a skull with hair.

2.

Night to night:
child walking toward me through burning maize
over the clean bones of those whose flesh
was lifted by *zopilotes* into heaven.

So that is how we ascend!
In the clawed feet of fallen angels
to be assembled again
in the workrooms of clouds.

3.

She rose from where they found her lying
not far from a water urn, leaving
herself behind on the ground

where they found her, holding her arms
before her as if she were asleep.

4.

Blue smoke rising from corncribs, the flap of wings.
On the walls of the city streets a *plague of initials.*

5.

Walking through a firelit river
to a burning house: dead Singer
sewing machine and piece of dress.

Outside a cashew tree wept
blackened cashews over lamina.

Outside paper fireflies rose to the stars.

6.

Bring penicillin if you can, you said, surgical tape,
a whetstone, mosquito repellent but not the aerosol kind.
Especially bring a syringe for sucking phlegm,
a knife, wooden sticks, a clamp, and plastic bags.

You will also need a bottle of cloud for anesthesia:
to sleep like the flight of a crane through colorless dreams.

7.

When a leech opens your flesh, it leaves a small volcano.
Always pour turpentine over your hair before going to sleep.

8.

Such experiences as these are forgotten
before memory intrudes.

The girl was found (don't say this)
with a man's severed head stuffed
into her where a child would have been.
No one knew who the man was.
Another of the dead.
So they had not, after all,
killed a pregnant girl.

9.

That sound in the brush?
A settling of wind in sorghum.

10.

If they capture you, talk.

Talk. Please, yes.
You heard me the first time.

You will be asked who you are.
Eventually, we are all asked who we are.

All who come
All who come into the world
All who come into the world are sent.
Open your curtain of spirit.

Your cinerary box was light, but filled with you it weighed eight pounds.
Nevertheless, we each wanted our turn carrying you up the mountain.
We passed the roofless chapel, the crater, the graves of the youngest,
the camping place, the secret paths, the impossible stone road.
We came upon the shivering trees where the magical foreign doctor
was said to dig out bullets with a penknife and supply the children
with iron by dipping rusty nails in water. We came upon the past,
where the holes were dug, and if you dug there now you'd fill quite a sack
with bones. We don't stop to dig there. We carried your box
to another place, not as far as we would have liked, but far enough,
where we all had our pictures taken with you, and then your box
posed with your former truck, that will now belong to the priest
you saved from prison. The truck seemed to know what had happened.
We spent a long time piling stones around the trees, even the mayor
who was once a fighter himself in these hills piled stones.
Then with cupped hands we tossed your remains into a coppice of cedars.
You flew a little, your soft ash flew, settling on the stones under the trees.
A camouflage moth alighted on the tree where most of you fell, and there
your friend worked his machete until a cross appeared, and within it
a Christ of sap and grain. The moth then vanished into the jacaranda
and dragonflies arrived, hovering, then from nowhere butterflies
rained into the coppice, blue mariposas, as they sometimes do
into the roofless chapel, and as dragonflies whirred above us,

a camouflage moth held still with its wings open, and the mariposas
rose and fell until all was dust and wings—you in flight—leaving
a life without a day not given to others, leaving us to stand
in a sunlit clearing of butterflies and ash where your soul is loosed.

We went down the Perfume River by dragon boat
as far as the pagoda of the three golden Buddhas.

Pray here. You can ask for happiness.
We light joss sticks, send votives downriver in paper sacks,

then have trouble disembarking from the boat.
Our bodies disembark, but our souls remain.

A thousand lanterns drift, a notebook opens in the dark
to a page where moonlight makes a sound.

These soldiers are decades from war now:
pewter-haired, steel-haired, a moon caught in plumeria.

We are like the clouds that pass and pass.
What does it matter then if we are not the same as clouds?

There was then the whir of stork wings, and bicycle chains ringing.
It is still now the way the air is still just before the mine explodes.

Once we fired at each other. Now we pass silence back and forth.
On the ten thousand graves, we lay chrysanthemum.

The lights across the water are the waking city.

The water shimmers with imaginary fish.

Not far from here lie the bones of conifers

washed from the sea and piled by wind.

Some mornings I walk upon them,

bone to bone, as far as the lighthouse.

A strange beetle has eaten most of the trees.

It may have come here on the ships playing

music in the harbor, or it was always here, a winged

jewel, but in the past was kept still by the cold

of a winter that no longer comes.

There is an owl living in the firs behind us, but he is white,

meant to be mistaken for snow burdening a bough.

They say he is the only owl remaining. I hear him at night

listening for the last of the mice and asking *who* of no other owl.

A BRIDGE

Behind us a sea-cliff, landfall, ahead the wind,
tar-smoke, the sea, a carrick.
We sway on a bridge between them
above a great shattering. We have left
the verge, our certainty, and walk across
a chasm to the cries of cormorants, fulmars,
the wings of mute swans singing in flight.
Below us bladder wrack, sea froth, and dulse,
sea against rocks in heave and salt, and between
bridge and sea an abyss we cross, as behind us
the headland recedes—cottages and boats, clouds and sheep,
a piping of oystercatchers dying out, and the callings
of kittiwakes preparing to leave their nesting ground.
The bridge rises and falls with our steps, moving in wind
so we must hold fast the ropes
once made of hides and the hair of cows' tails
hoisted over the silvering salmon as they leapt
into bag nets too heavy to lift, hauled
across this very bridge that rings in wind
like ship's rigging, volary of rock pipits,
bazaar of guillemots, colony of puffins,
and in the blackest water below us ghosts
of salmon, empty nets, and on the carrick
ruins of boats, nets, buoys, and a fisherman's bothy.

We have only to keep walking for the bridge to go on.

The carrick is a foothold in the distance, a stone in time.

When we reach it, not only may the salmon return

but you will be alive again, wake me when we reach the carrick.

THE END OF SOMETHING

That summer we lived in the hills near San Gersolè,
where a saint sleeps holding poppies in a glass coffret,
about to unbutton what would have been her wedding dress.
Other than this not much is known about the saint.

This is the church of a thousand years: vineyards,
hummingbirds, swifts, chicory, swallows, bindweed,
and the ringing of bells for liturgy, births, and deaths,
with a flock of bells to tell the village of war or its end.
Mornings we wake to light upon stone, much as the sisters
who lived here in the fourteenth century came from sleep,
swallows foraging from an eternity of eaves.

On the last day, we have our lunch of figs under the lindens.
The lemons are nearly ripe, hanging like ornaments from a lemon branch.
This isn't our last day, she says. Tomorrow is our last day.
As proof, she offers time singing in the darkness of time.

We are trying to climb to the ruins when my heart gives way.
When my heart gives way in the poppy field I have to turn back.
Before turning back, I press a few poppies in a book.
Before turning back, I take a photograph of no one
standing in a poppy field. I am myself standing.
I ask my mother, thousands of miles away, to help me back.

EARLY LIFE

In *Le Détroit du Lac Érié*, five years after the end of war, I was born.

My father's naval uniform hung among our coats and his white cap
flung into the sea at war's end still then floated on the waves there.

My father built a house for us, working in the dark after his factory shift.
One night a long-buried woman appeared, all fog and bones, passing

through a wall he'd yet to finish. Later we hung a mirror there
and from time to time the fog woman stood behind the mirror looking out.

Beneath a nearby house, there was a cellar where escaping slaves once were
hidden.
An underground railroad carried them through a tunnel beneath the fields.

In the mornings the fields hummed their readiness.

In the orchard, apples and apricots appeared in the trees, and in the garden
sudden red cabbage, blue-leaved lilies, endive, and wandering mint.

Over the field crawled squash vine and blossom until a row of berry
canes stood in a cloud of bees, and lettuces opened in watery light.

When Anna was with us, pillows of bread rose in bowls and soup boiled the windows blind. Anna was from the old country. This was the new one.

Many sentences began with *Be quiet now*, in voices like birches in snow. They began their stories *when the war ended*. Never when the war began.

There is no album for these, no white script on black
paper, no dates stamped in a border, no sleeve, no fire,
no one has written on the back from left to right.
Your hair has not yet fallen out nor grown back—
girl walking toward you out of childhood
not yet herself, having not yet learned to recite
before others, and who would never wish to stand
on a lighted proscenium, even in a darkened house,
but would rather dig a hole in a field and cover herself
with barn wood, earth, and hay, to be as quiet as plums turning.
There is no calendar, no month, no locket, but your name
is called and called in the early storm. No one finds
you, no one ever finds you. Not in a small grave
dug by a child as a hiding place, nor years
later in the ship's hold. Not in the shelter, nor high
on the roof as the man beside you leapt, not
in a basket crossing a vineyard, nor in a convent
kitchen on the last night, as a saint soon to be
murdered told you how to live your life,
never found you walking in the ruins of the blown
barracks, wading in the flooded camp, taking cover
in the machinist's shop, or lighting every votive
in the Cathedral of Saint Just, with its vaulted
choir and transept, a wall of suffering souls.
It was just as Brecht wrote, wasn't it? "You came

in a time of unrest when hunger reigned.
You came to the people in a time of uprising
and you rose with them. So the time
passed away which on earth was given you."
Gather in your sleep the ripened plums.
Stay behind in the earth when your name is called.

VISITATION

On the nativity tree, a tiny lute, a French horn and painted egg,
a crèche carved from olive wood, a trumpeting angel. The Cossack
in a red tunic dances between a bird's nest and some Eiffel Towers.
In the iced window, a cathedral shivers in mist as bits of torn cloud
float toward the spires. There are also boats sailing
in the window, and a city resembling Dresden or Hamburg after the war.
Anna is there, crocheting smoke, not speaking English anymore, as if
English had put out her memory like a broom on a fire. The snows
drift to the roof of the house, so it is no longer possible to open the door.
She tells us that on this night in her village, they would carry home
a live carp wrapped in paper that had just been swimming in a barrel.
The fish would silver the snow and have its life taken by a sharp ax.
The potatoes that had grown eyes in the cellar would be brought up
and baked with the fish, and there would be beet soup, bread, and wine
made from mulberries. Something would be given to each of them,
a thing they needed but didn't want, and then they would sleep
as if in a boat at sea with the bright carp swimming through the snow
of their thoughts. Then she would be off, tunneling through the drifts
as only a spirit could tunnel, leaving behind a coin purse, a crystal broach,
a holy card with her own birth and death dates so we would know
she hadn't visited us, that her satin-pillowed coffin lay still in the ground.
Nevertheless, the tinsel flickered as she passed, the lighthouse sent
its signal to the boats, and the sheep bounded over the fir branch
tufted with wool, and in every glass bulb, there we were—
children descended from her on a winter night.

IN TIME OF WAR

And so we stayed, night after night awake
until the moon fell behind the blackened cypress,
and bats returned to their caverns having gorged
on the night air, and all remained still until the hour
of rising, when the headless woman was no longer seen
nor a ghostly drum heard, nor anyone taking
the form of mist or a fiddler, and the box never opened
by itself, nor were there whispers or other sounds, no rustling
dress or pet ape trapped in a secret passage, but there was
labored breathing, and unseen hands leafing through
the pages of a visitor's book, and above the ruins a girl
in white lace, and five or more candles floating,
and someone did see a white dog bound into a nearby
wood, but there were neither bagpipes nor smiling skull,
no skeletons piled in the oubliette, and there was,
as it turned out, no yellow monkey, no blood
leaking from a slit throat, and no one saw
a woman carrying the severed head,
but there were children standing on their own
graves and there was the distant rumble of cannon.

LOST POEM

I'm searching for a poem I read years ago. It was written by Cavafy, I thought, but reading through Cavafy again I can't find this poem. I don't recall the title, but there is a road in the poem, and a bridge, and a city near the sea. There are many souls and hungers, figs, demons, imaginary silence, and hidden phrases that have to do with secret assignations. The poem is said to have been written on the uncut pages of a dream. In one version, the olive trees go up in smoke but the bridge survives. In another, the city itself is lost, and there is no road. It is a war poem then, and that is why it is not to be found in the collected works of Cavafy.

It begins with a word as small as the cry of Athena's owl.
An ache in the cage of breath, as when we say *can hardly breathe.*
In sleep, we see our name on a stone, for instance.
Or while walking in the rain among graves we feel watched.
Others are still *coming into our lives.* They come, they go out.
Some speak quietly beside us on the bench near where koi swim.
At night, there is a light sound of wings brushing the walls.
Not now is what it sounds like. Or two other words.
But they are the same passerines as live in the stone eaves,
as forage in the air toward night. To see them one must not be looking.

SOUFFRANCE

I think of you in that sea of graves beyond the city,
where many stones have been left, among them,

mine: a little piece of dolomite to weigh down a slip of paper.
I would have put your gloves and umbrella in the coffin,

along with one more morning in Berlin with Tanya, an hour
of pigeons rising around you, lilacs wrapped in news

stories, a minute at the barricades, another riding
on your father's shoulders through the garlic fields, even cigarettes

left over from the occupation I would have placed there.
Instead, this notebook, a pen full of ink, and that short

poem by Hölderlin you loved, so you could go up in smoke
together: you, the notebook, the pen, the poem by Hölderlin.

In the aftermath, you are emulsion on paper, a corpse listening beneath
the ground to a train passing through a polaroid of clouds.

It was Joseph who said that for all eternity, Venice would happen only once.
You are a ghost then, following a ghost back through its only life.

Or as you say now: there were many cities, but never a city twice.

SANCTUARY

Ce voyage, je voulais le refaire—
This journey, I would like to make again—

Light pealed, bell-like, through the canopy. Long ago or seems so.

Then the ghost of a deer and crows flapping through smoke.

She made a poultice for me of herbs and mud to suck the poison from the
    boil.

And then she went into a mahogany coffin. As there were then.

Mornings, horses cantered through ground fog having broken loose.

So I would go out for them, bridles in hand, with no one awake.

The closer I came to them, the further they moved away.

Following them through the clouds is a journey I would make again.

UNINHABITED

night moaning in an open flue
wings along the chimney wall

the house as it was, as winter drew
frost's white face on the glass

and you, as then you were
as old as you would ever be,

playing Schubert in the air,
on the invisible keys

of a piano that wasn't there—

for the one who vanished near Voronezh
for "shovels of smoke in the air"

for the wristwatch missing in the river
from the walker who slipped from the edge

for a suitcase left in the Pyrenees
for spectacles crushed at Portbou

for the shawl of stars that was night
when the last of them spoke to you.

CLOUDS

A whip-poor-will brushed
her wing along the ground
a moment ago, fifty years
in the orchard where my father
kept pear and plum,
a decade of peach trees
and Antonovka's apples
whose seeds come
from Russia by ship
under clouds islanding
a window very past
where also went
the soul of my mother
in a boat with blossoming
sails like apple petals
in wind fifty years at once.

PASSAGE

a boat in snow
a boat with a cargo
of refuse moored on a field
water chiming into a bowl
the long hum of a gong in wind
and from the sickroom a death rattle
a falling back as if through clouds
someone in the room
seen only by the dying one
there, just there, in the room
in the past, the window sash raised,
the curtain flared
as a girl's skirt in wind
there would be a pitcher
of water on the night table—
some kind of game the children
would be playing would be heard
like a call from tree to tree
during apple harvest

In the library of night, from the darkness of ink
on paper, there is a whispering heard book to book,
from *Great Catastrophe* and *The World of Silence*
to *The Encyclopedia of Ephemera*, a history having
to do with aerial leaflets, air raid papers,
bills of mortality, birth certificates and blotting papers,
child lost-and-found forms, donor cards, erratum slips,
execution broadsides "liberally spattered with errors of all kinds"
sold by vendors at public hangings, *funeralia*, with drawings
of skeletons digging graves and inviting us to accompany
the corpse of x to the church of y, gift coupons, greeting cards,
housekeeping accounts, ice papers to place in windows
for the delivery of blocks of ice, jury papers, keepsakes,
lighthouse dues slips for all ships entering or leaving ports,
marriage certificates, news bills, notices to quit, oaths, paper
dolls, plague papers, playing cards, quack advertisements,
ration papers, razor blade wrappers, reward posters,
slave papers, songbooks, tax stamps, touring maps,
union labels and vice cards left in telephone boxes,
warrants and watch papers used to keep the movements
of the pocket watches under repair free of dust,
wills and testaments, xerography, yearbooks, and the zoetrope
disk, also known as the wheel of life, wherein figures painted
in a rotating drum are perceived to move, faster and faster,
whether dancing, flying, or dying in the whirl of time.

THEOLOGOS

For a third year, we are living on AERIA THASSOS, island of marble and
    pines,
marble the quietest of stones, pines the first tree after a fire.

Marble the stone of the dead, the stone of the sleeping face.

This is an island of exiles and therefore pure,
its sea flocked with boats in the day hours.

In the swells the *Evanthoulla* rises and falls, a boat alive and awake.

In a clear dawn the islands of Samothraki, Limnos, and Lesvos are visible.
Later in the morning there is too much light.

You may catch birds in nets, the first poet wrote, *but you cannot in nets
catch their song.*

These fragments of Archilochus were found on a slip of paper used
to wrap a mummy.

He lived here, it was said, on an island that *lies in the sea / like the backbone of
    an ass,*
making the first iambs.

He wrote *sparks in wheat.*
And it seems, from accounts, he fought and fornicated mostly.

Later in the day, Kyrios Stamatis takes the boat
to think with him on open sea, setting his nets.

Sea-wind fills the olives.
A ship crosses the seam of air and sea.

Hillocks and canyons of cloud,
light-strewn, castle-walled, shore and cirrus.

This is where the skinned goat turned on the spit.
This is where we knelt on walnut leaves to be blessed.

MOURNING

A peacock on an olive branch looks beyond
the grove to the road, beyond the road to the sea,
blank-lit, where a sailboat anchors to a cove.
As it is morning, below deck a man is pouring water into a cup,
listening to the radio-talk of the ships: barges dead
in the calms awaiting port call, pleasure boats whose lights
hours ago went out, fishermen setting their nets for mullet,
as summer tavernas hang octopus to dry on their lines,
whisper smoke into wood ovens, sweep the terraces
clear of night, putting the music out with morning
light, and for the breadth of an hour it is possible
to consider the waters of this sea *wine-dark*, to remember
that there was no word for blue among the ancients,
but there was the whirring sound before the oars
of the great triremes sang out of the seam of world,
through pine-sieved winds silvered by salt flats until
they were light enough to pass for breath from the heavens,
troubled enough to fell ships and darken thought—
then as now the clouds pass, roosters sleep in their huts,
the sea flattens under glass air, but there is nothing to hold us there:
not the quiet of marble nor the luff of sail, fields of thyme,
a vineyard at harvest, and the sea filled with the bones of those
in flight from wars east and south, our wars, their remains
scavenged on the seafloor and in its caves, belongings now
a flotsam washed to the rocks. Stand here and look

into the distant haze, there where the holy mountain

with its thousand monks wraps itself in shawls of rain,

then look to the west, where the rubber boats tipped

into the tough waves. Rest your eyes there, remembering the words

of Anacreon, himself a refugee of war, who appears

in the writings of Herodotus:

How the waves of the sea kiss the shore!

For if the earth is a camp and the sea

an ossuary of souls, light your signal fires

wherever you find yourselves.

Come the morning, launch your boats.

TRANSPORT

Oxen-yoked carts go with us, and also bicycle rickshaws,
three-wheeled carts, small trucks, taxis and cooled private cars,
human-yoked carts piled with tea and textiles, and along
the way they toot their horns. To pass on the right,
you toot your horn, also to pass on the left or pull ahead.
Even the loping oxen understand the music.
We are told—is it true?—that if our driver struck
a man on foot, we should run away before the car
is torched by the crowd and its driver killed.
This thought became taxis burning in sleep.
The newness of the car determines our distance from the world.
Behind smoked windows, with the air *on*,
it is possible to travel at great distance
from all that is about us: bathers by the roadside pouring
cold pails over soaped flesh, smoke rising from long metal
stoves, women stirring pots, sadhus and other holy ones,
with their infinite paths to God. On foot then. Go on foot.

EARLY CONFESSION

If I had never walked the snow fields, heard the iced birch,
leant against wind hard toward distant houses, ever distant,
wind in the coat, snow over the boot tops, supper fires
in windows far across the stubbly farms, none of them
my house until the end, the last, and late, always late, despite how early
I'd set off wearing gloves of glass, a coat standing up by itself.
If I had never reached the house, but instead lain down in the drifts
to finish a dream, if I had finished, would I have
reached the rest of my life, here, now, with you whispering:
must not sleep, not rest, must not take flight, must wake.

In this archipelago of thought a fog descends, horns of ships to unseen
    ships, a year
passing overhead, the cry of a year not knowing where, someone standing
    in the aftermath

who once you knew, the one you were then, a little frisson of recognition,
and then just like that—gone, and no one for hours, a sound you thought
    you heard

but in the waking darkness is not heard again, two sharp knocks on the
    door, death
it was, you said, but now nothing, the islands, places you have been, the sea
    the uncertain,

full of ghosts calling out, lost as they are, no one you knew in your life, the
    moon above
the whole of it, like the light at the bottom of a well opening in iced air

where you have gone under and come back, light, no longer tethered
to your own past, and were it not for the weather of trance, of haze and
    murk, you could see

everything at once: all the islands, every moment you have lived or place

you have been,

without confusion or bafflement, and you would be one person. You would

be one person again.

> *J'ai rapporté du désespoir un panier si petit, mon amour, qu'on a*
> *pu le tresser en osier.*
> *I brought from despair a basket so small, my love, that it might*
> *have been woven of willow.*

RENÉ CHAR

to speak is not yet to have spoken,

the not-yet of a white realm of nothing left

neither for itself nor another

a no-longer already there, along with the arrival of what has been

light and the reverse of light

terror as walking blind along the breaking sea, body in whom I lived

the not-yet of death darkening what it briefly illuminates

an unknown place as between languages

back and forth, breath to breath as a calm

in the surround rises, fireflies in lindens, an ache of pine

you have yourself within you

yourself, you have her, and there is nothing

that cannot be seen

open then to the coming of what comes

DEDICATIONS AND NOTES

The title of this collection is from Robert Duncan's poem "Poetry, a Natural Thing."

"Museum of Stones" is in memory of Hugh Anthony Sloan, 1953–2007.

"Exile," "Fisherman," and "For Ilya at Tsarskoye Selo" are for Ilya Kaminsky.

"The Lost Suitcase," "The Last Bridge," and "Elegy for an Unknown Poet" are in memory of Daniel Simko, 1959–2004, poet and translator of Georg Trakl.

"The Refuge of Art" is for Ashley Ashford-Brown.

"A Room" is in memory of Robert Creeley, who gave us the glass cubes. Chapter titles are from David Hume.

"The Ghost of Heaven" and "Ashes to Guazapa" are in memory of Leonel Gómez, 1939–2009.

"Hue: From a Notebook" is for Kevin Bowen, Bruce Weigl, Nguyen Ba Chung, and Larry Heinemann.

"A Bridge": A *bothy* is a ruined hut restored for use by trekkers and fishermen.

"The End of Something" is for Lise Goett.

"Lost Poem" is for Lars Gustaf Andersson.

"Theologos": Archilochus was a Greek lyric poet from the island of Paros, 680–645 BC. This poem is for Stamatis Kouzis of Thassos.

"Toward the End" is for Eryk Hanut.

"What Comes" is for Barbara Cully.

ACKNOWLEDGMENTS

With gratitude to the editors of the following publications, in which these poems first appeared: *Boston Review, Kenyon Review, The Nation, The New Yorker, Poetry, Poetry International, Poetry London, Salmagundi, Province-town Arts, Best American Poetry,* and *World Literature Today.* Broadsides of "Museum of Stones," "What Comes," and "Light of Sleep" were published by Folger Shakespeare Library, the Rose O'Neill Literary House, Kore Press, and the Jack Sinclair Letterpress Lab at the University of Arizona, respectively.

Dedicated to my father, Michael Joseph Sidlosky, and my mother, the late Louise Blackford Sidlosky (1926–2013).

What You Have Heard Is True
A Memoir of Witness and Resistance

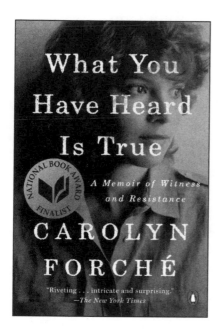

Carolyn Forché is twenty-seven when the mysterious stranger appears on her doorstep. The relative of a friend, he is charming, brilliant, and rumored to be a revolutionary. He has driven from El Salvador to invite Forché to visit and learn about his country. Captivated for reasons she doesn't fully understand, she accepts and becomes enmeshed in something beyond her comprehension. *What You Have Heard Is True* is a devastating and visionary memoir about a young woman's brave choice to engage with horror in order to help others.

"Once Forché's story gathers momentum, it's hard to let the narrative go. . . . Riveting." —*The New York Times*

PENGUIN BOOKS